KU-068-120

SOUTHWARK LIBRARIES
SK 2757858 5

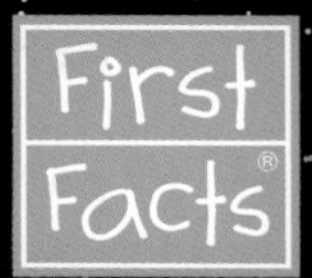

THE MOON AND OTHER SATELLITES

by Ellen Labrecque

a Capstone company — publishers for children

Raintree is an imprint of Capstone Global Library Limited, a company incorporated in England and Wales having its registered office at 264 Banbury Road, Oxford, OX2 7DY – Registered company number: 6695582

www.raintree.co.uk
myorders@raintree.co.uk

Edited by Hank Musolf
Designed by Kyle Grenz
Media Research by Jo Miller
Production by Kathy McColley
Originated by Capstone Global Library Ltd
Printed and bound in India

978 1 4747 8683 6 (hardback)
978 1 4747 8693 5 (paperback)

British Library Cataloguing in Publication Data
A full catalogue record for this book is available from the British Library.

Acknowledgements
We would like to thank the following for permission to reproduce photographs: NASA; JPL-Caltech, 7, W. Liller, 19; Shutterstock: BlueRingMedia, 9, Cristian Cestaro, Cover, Dotted Yeti, 17 (Both), jakkapan, 15, kdshutterman, 5, kdshutterman, 21, Korionov, 22, Nevada31, 11, psoundphoto, 9, robert_s, 8, Siberian Art, 13
Design Elements
Capstone; Shutterstock: Alex Mit, Dimonika, Kanata

Contents

Meet the moons

What is one of the brightest objects in our night sky? The moon! The moon doesn't make its own light. It **reflects** the sun's light.

FAR-OUT FACT

Twelve people have visited our moon. It is the only other space object apart from Earth that people have stood on.

reflect to return light from an object; the moon reflects light from the sun

The Earth has one moon. Other planets can have more than one moon. Moons are **satellites**. They **orbit** a planet or a star. Let's learn about the many moons in our **universe**.

orbit to travel around an object in space

satellite object in space that moves around a planet or a star

universe everything that exists, including the Earth, the stars and all of space

Earth's moon

Our moon formed more than 4 billion years ago. Scientists think it formed when a giant **asteroid** hit the Earth. The big crash sent many bits into space. Over time, the bits formed into the moon.

FAR-OUT FACT

The moon is much smaller than Earth. Fifty moons could fit inside our planet.

asteroid a rocky object in space

The moon's surface is covered in craters. A crater is a bowl-shaped pit. The craters formed when asteroids slammed into the moon. The moon does not have an **atmosphere** like Earth to protect itself.

atmosphere gases that surround planets or other objects in space

We only see one side of the moon from Earth. We call this side the near side. The other is called the far side. We never see the far side from Earth.

The moon takes 27 days to orbit the Earth. It spins slowly as it orbits. It spins just once during the 27 days. Earth's gravity keeps the same side of the moon always facing us.

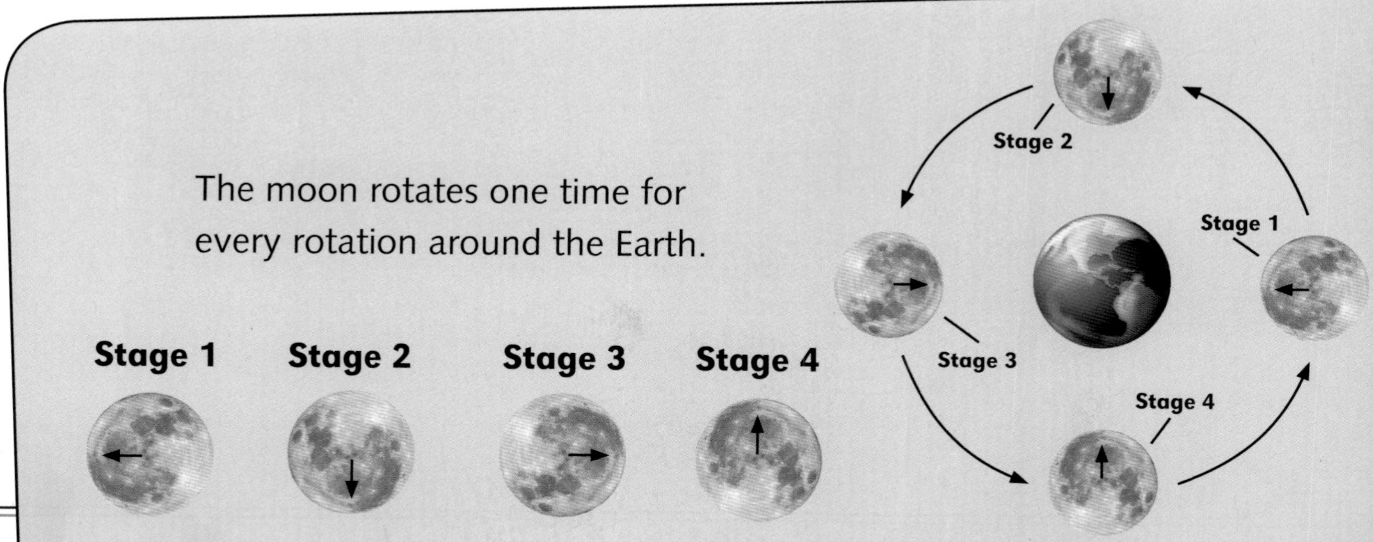

The moon rotates one time for every rotation around the Earth.

The moon is a giant ball of rock. But from Earth, it can look like it changes shape. This is because of the way sunlight hits it. Sometimes the sun lights up the whole moon. At other times it lights up just a sliver. Sometimes it hardly lights up any shape at all. These changes are called the phases of the moon.

Phases of the moon

New moon

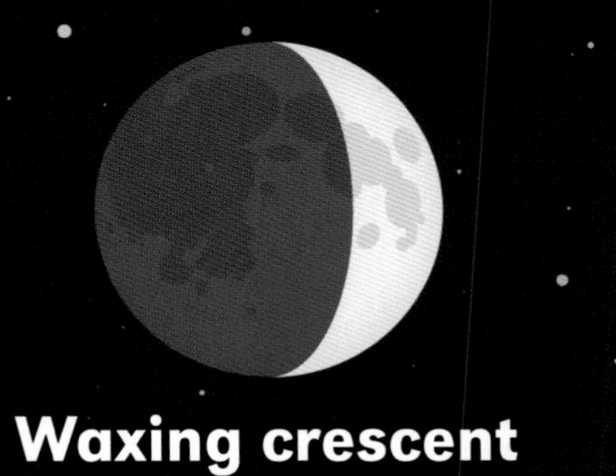

Waxing crescent

First quarter

Waxing gibbous

Full moon

Waning gibbous

Last quarter

Waning crescent

New moon

Eclipse

An eclipse happens when one object in space moves into the shadow of another object.

A lunar eclipse is an eclipse of the moon. The Earth moves in between the moon and the sun. The Earth blocks the sunlight that usually is reflected by the moon. This can only happen when we see a full moon from Earth.

FAR-OUT FACT

Luna is the Latin word for moon.

Lunar eclipse

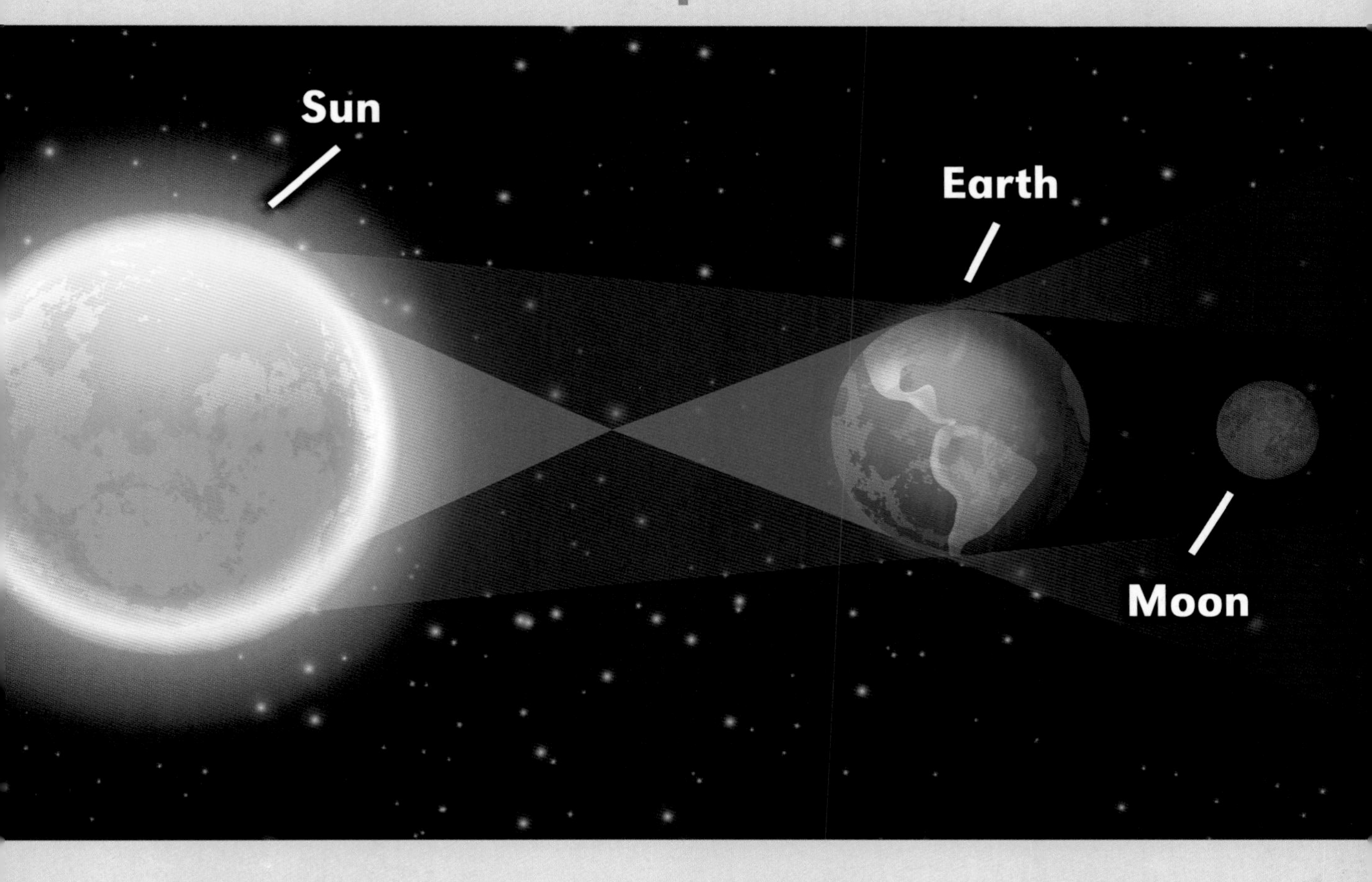

A moon is always smaller than the planet it is orbiting.

The tide is high

Did you know the moon changes the ocean's **tides**? When the ocean is at its highest point, it is called a high tide. When it is at its lowest point, it is called a low tide. The rise and fall of the oceans is a result of the moon's pull. We have two low tides and two high tides every day.

tide the rise or fall of sea level at a certain place

Other moons

Nobody knows how many moons are in the universe. We know that there are 181 moons in our solar system. Our solar system is made up of the sun and the planets that orbit it. Earth is one of these planets. The giant planet Jupiter has the most moons. It has 67.

The four planets Jupiter, Saturn, Uranus and Neptune have more than 140 moons between them.

Jupiter and some of its many moons

Active volcanoes

One of Jupiter's moons is named Io. Io has many active volcanoes on it. Its surface is covered in **lava**. Some of the lava that erupts out of the volcanoes goes many kilometres high.

lava liquid rock that spews from a volcano

Other satellites

Apart from moons, other satellites are in space. Asteroids also orbit other planets and the sun. **Comets** orbit around planets too. The most famous comet is called Halley's Comet. It orbits the sun every 76 years. We last saw Halley's Comet from Earth in 1986. We could next see it in 2061!

comet object in space that has dust and gas around it that form a tail

Comets speed through outer space.

Look up!

Don't forget to look up when you are outside at night. Is it a full moon? Is it a half moon? Is it only a crescent? Maybe you can't even see it at all.

Space is an amazing place. Today astronauts still visit the moon to study it. Maybe one day you will go to the moon!

Glossary

asteroid rocky object in space

atmosphere gases that surround planets or other objects in space

comet object in space that has dust and gas around it that form a tail

lava the liquid rock that spews from a volcano

orbit to travel around an object in space

reflect to return light from an object; the moon reflects light from the sun

satellite an object in space that moves around a planet or a star

tide the rise or fall of sea level at a certain place

universe everything that exists, including the Earth, the stars and all of space

Find out more

Big Book of Stars and Planets (Big Books), Emily Bone (Usborne, 2016)

First Space Encyclopedia: A First Reference Book for Children (DK, 2016)

Phases of the Moon (Cycles of Nature), Catherine Ipcizade (Raintree, 2019)

Websites

NASA Science: Earth's Moon
moon.nasa.gov/about/in-depth/

Windows to the Universe: Our Solar System
www.windows2universe.org/our_solar_system/solar_system.html

Comprehension questions

- How do the phases of the moon occur?
- How do scientists think craters formed on the moon?
- How does the moon affect the sea?

Index